Ritual Implements, Tools & Objects of Chinese Buddhism

Harry Leong

Yuan Kuang Buddhist Publications

Taiwan, 2001

Yuan Kuang Buddhist Publications
No. 11 Lane 888, Section 1 Sheng Te Road
Chungli, Taiwan, R.O.C.

Contact Information
Harry Leong
P. O. Box 142
New York, NY 10002
U.S.A.
harry_leong@hotmail.com

ISBN 957-8896-22-0

Printed in Taiwan, Republic Of China.

Contents

Plate 1

Shakyamuni Buddha

v

Plate 2

Bodhisattva Thousand-hands Avalokiteshvara/Guan-yin   vii

七俱胝佛母大準提真言
讚曰　稽首皈依蘇悉帝　頭面頂禮七俱胝
唯願慈悲垂加護　我今稱讚大準提

心月梵字觀念之時。字字五色光明。圖附後。

偈云。唵中遮那佛。折南是大輪。隸西南不動。主西觀世音。
隸西北胃索。準北準提尊。握東北金剛。婆東伊迦神。
洞東南囉日。心月九聖字。即作三摩地。名瑜伽觀行。

Plate 3

Bodhisattva Chundi Avalokiteshvara/Guan-yin　　ix

南無地藏王菩薩

Plate 4

Bodhisattva Kshitigarbha/Di-zhang flanked by two attendants xi

Notes on Abbreviations

Chn: Chinese

Jpn: Japanese

Tib: Tibetan

Skt: Sanskrit

BCE: Before the Common Era

CE: Common Era

Acknowledgements

A special mention of grateful acknowledgement and sincerest thanks is given to Rev. Shing Chien Shih. Without her unselfish help and constant guidance, and not to mention all her work in Chinese input, book design and layout, and general production assistance, this work would never have been possible. Thus, I am indebted to her for all her invaluable help.

I also would like to express my appreciation to my Chinese refuge master, Venerable Fa Yun, for his unwavering compassion and support throughout the time while I was working on this book.

In addition, I also thank Rev. Shing Yuan Shih who speedily provided on such short notice some of the pictures from Yuan Kuang Monastery that were used in this book. Also, I am grateful to Venerable Si Chen, Rev. Ming-yu Shi and Rev. Pin-dao Shi for graciously lending to me their ritual objects so that I could photograph them. Michael Chee kindly assisted in computer image re-editing of all pictures and Gil Leong also helped in some of the photography for this book at a time when it was greatly needed.

The following publications, listed in alphabetical order, are also dutifully acknowledged for the use of some of their magazine photos.

B.A.U.S. Magazine (美佛慧訊/*Mei Fo Hui Xun*)

Bo Lin Chan Si (柏林禪寺)

Bodhedrum (菩提樹/*Pu Ti Shu*)

Buddhism in Hong Kong (香港佛教/*Xiang Gang Fo Jiao*)

Ch'ien Fo Shan (千佛山/*Qian Fo Shan*)

Chinese Buddhism Monthly (中國佛教/*Zhong Guo Fo Jiao*)

Humanity (人生/*Ren Sheng*)

Kuan Hong Fo Jiao Yi Shu Zhong Xin Mu Lu (寬宏佛教藝術中心目錄)

Ling Yen Xiao Cong Shu (靈嚴小叢書)

Miao Lin (妙林)

The Lion's Roar (獅子吼/*Shi Zi Hou*)

Universal Gate (普門/*Pu Men*)

Universal Magazine (十方/*Shi Fang*)

Yuan Guang Xin Zhi (圓光新誌)

Preface

Over the course of centuries, the Chinese Buddhist tradition has evolved a wide range of ceremonial implements and practice tools that serve as supports for the unique practice of the Chinese Buddhist religion. Oftentimes, visitors to Chinese Buddhist temples in Asia and overseas countries may feel curious about these paraphernalia that they observe in the daily usage of Chinese Buddhist monastics and wonder as to what their meanings are.

Because there has not been any work in the English language that explains the meanings and symbolism of these various implements, tools and objects, it is the attempt of this book to humbly do so. However, this is by no means to be considered an exhaustive study.

Footnotes have been added to certain entries to further elucidate the introductions in more detail for those who may be interested in a more extensive explanation of how the meanings of these objects tie in with Buddhist teachings and doctrine.

The Chinese terms in this book are romanized using the Pinyin system of transliteration (as opposed to the more older Wades-Giles system) because Pinyin is fast becoming the system used as the academic standard. All corresponding terms available in Sanskrit and other languages, if known, are given without any diacritical marks and are rendered as best according to their phonetic spelling (for the sake of cross reference for interested readers). The only exception to this convention might be some more familiar or well-established terms in Buddhism which in that case were left in their more popular spelling.

Also, readers should understand that wherever the word "monk" may appear alone in this book is done purely for the sake of maintaining brevity but really refers to both monks and nuns (male and female members of the Buddhist monastic order) and that there is no purposeful intention to be gender-specific. The same applies to the use of any masculine pronouns in this book.

If there are any errors in this book, they are entirely my own and I humbly ask that those who are more knowledgeable than me to correct my mistakes. Hopefully, if even a few people find interest in the information presented in this work, I will feel that this book has served its purpose.

Harry Leong
New York, USA
October 2000

Ritual Implements, Tools & Objects
of Chinese Buddhism

Shrine & Altar Objects

Banner · Pennant
Candle · Candlestick Holder
Canopy · Parasol
Incense
Incense Vessel
Oil Lamp
Pagoda · Stupa
Prayer Cushion

Banner · Pennant
幢 · 幡

Chn: *chuang · fan*

Jpn: *do · ban*

Tib: *gyaltsen*

Skt: *dhvaja · ketu · pataka*

Banners and pennants are generally regarded as signs of leadership, sovereignty, and virtue of the Buddha's Teachings. They are often used as hanging ornaments to decorate and adorn the interior of Buddhist shrines and temples. They vary in form and design but the most commonly seen in Chinese Buddhist temples are those that are long and rectangular.

Most often, banners and pennants include auspicious designs and symbols and have individual streamers, ribbons, or pieces of jade that dangle from their periphery.

Horizontal banners that are hung across the top of altars have inscriptions of popular Buddhist proclamations or adages used in Chinese temple decoration.[1] Vertical banners that are hung on both sides of a sacred image often bear words hailing the name of the buddha or bodhisattva or words that extol the merits of the particular deity. Vertical banners and pennants can also

be attached to curved handles that are carried by attendant bearers in ceremonial processions.

In Buddhist imagery and art, the banner or pennant is also commonly seen. For example, it is one of the many sacred objects carried by Bodhisattva Avalokiteshvara in some of her representations.[2]

---

1. For example, popular phrases written on temple banners at the top of altars are *Fo Guang Pu Zhao* (佛光普照/ Universal Illumination by the Buddha's Radiance) and *Wan De Zhuang Yan* (萬德莊嚴/ Adornment of Ten-Thousand Virtues).

2. See also Plate 3 for an example of Chundi Avalokiteshvara/Guan-yin (準提菩薩/ *zhun-ti-guan-yin*), a special esoteric form of this bodhisattva, carrying a banner in one of her many hands.

Candle · Candlestick Holder

蠟燭 · 燭台

Chn: *la-zhu · zhu-tai*

A candle, like an oil-lamp (see also *Oil Lamp*), feeds a burning flame which in Buddhism represents the illumination of Wisdom. The candlestick holder serves to hold the candle in place and to elevate its height so that the burning flame can produce a better effect of radiance. Candlestick holders can have various designs incorporating the forms

of lotus flowers, auspicious animals, and other aesthetic and symbolic images. They can be made of various substances including any type of metal or alloy, wood and stone.

Traditionally, candles (and the candlestick holders) are one of the three basic objects that are always placed on shrine tables and offering platforms. The other two basic objects are the incense vessel and a pair of flower vases. Candles are always placed in pairs on the altar table on both sides of the incense vessel.

The candle was probably a later development that came after the use of the oil-lamp and was gradually adopted as an important item for placement in shrines and on offering platforms.

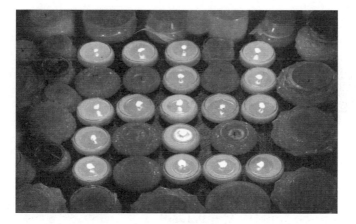

Canopy · Parasol

傘 · 蓋

Chn: *san · gai*

Tib: *labre*

Skt: *chattra*

The canopy, or parasol, is used in Buddhism as a symbol of honor, protection, and rank. It is a covering hung by strings or carried on a pole above an exalted personage or sacred object.

The canopy and parasol are similar, but they are used differently. The parasol is mobile and is constructed much like a regular umbrella with a central handle and is used to shield a Buddhist monk

during ceremonial events. An attendant bearer carries the parasol over the monk as an honorific symbol and follows him as he walks. The parasol can also be used to shield a sacred object or image in ceremonial events.

The canopy does not have a central handle like the parasol but is instead suspended in the air by strings or chords attached from the ceiling. Suspended canopies are seen in temples where they are hung above buddha and bodhisattva images.

 The fabric of the canopy and parasol is usually silk or satin stretched over a frame and embroidered with auspicious designs. Canopies and parasols can have ribbons or streamers that dangle from the periphery of its outer edge and some may have special symbols like the cintamani[1] mounted at the top. Some special canopies or parasols are constructed of very thin fine wood and instead of being circular, are sexagonal or octagonal in form. The use of canopies in adorning the images of buddhas and bodhisattvas are also said to bring about the merit of lengthening one's lifespan.

The religious symbolism of the canopy and parasol in Buddhism evolved from the ancient Indian custom of using the parasol as a sign of wealth, status or royalty.

The parasol is also seen in Buddhist art. For example, it is one of the objects carried by Bodhisattva Chundi Avalokiteshvara/Guan-yin. In Buddhist drawings, the canopy or parasol is sometimes seen magically floating over the head of the Buddha.

---

1. The *cintamani* (*chintamani*) (如意珠/ *ru-yi-zhu*) is the *wish-fulfilling jewel* in Buddhism and looks like a pearl or flaming jewel.

Incense

香

Chn: *xiang*

Jpn: *ko*

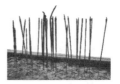

Incense is the principal offering substance used by Buddhist devotees in venerating the buddhas and bodhisattvas at Buddhist shrines. Incense that is fragrant and pure is considered especially worthy of being offered as a sign of homage and respect. The soft fragrance of incense can also help to bring about a meditative environment by inducing in the practitioner a serene and reverent mind. In addition, incense can be used to purify the air, dispel bad odors, and repel insects.[1]

The most common form of incense used by the Chinese is the straight incense stick that is inserted vertically into a vessel containing ash or rice. Very long sticks of incense that can burn for longer periods of time are also called *immortality incense* (仙香/*xian-xiang*) or *longevity incense* (長壽香/*chang-shou-xiang*).

Another popular type of incense used by the Chinese are incense coils that are spiral in shape. Incense coils are suspended from the ceiling or

may be placed on a vertical post over a circular tray so that each successive outer and larger spiral hangs lower than the preceding one, its diameter smaller towards the top and greater towards the bottom. The end of the outermost spiral at the bottom is lit and the incense coil burns slowly in circles until it reaches the top and

center. Incense coils burn for longer periods of time than straight incense sticks. This type of incense is also called *dish incense* (盤香/*pan-xiang*) because of its circular shape resembling a dish. They are usually positioned over a dish or tray that catches the falling ash.

A type of incense used for more elaborate ceremonies are pieces of fragrant, resinous incense wood that have been cut into short thin pieces and are burnt with incense powder. Incense wood, unlike the other common forms of incense mentioned above that are

made by solidifying together incense powder, are actually pieces of aromatic wood chips. The most common types of incense wood are sandalwood (檀香木/*tan-xiang-mu*) and aloeswood (沉香木/*chen-xiang-mu*). Because this kind of incense is made by cutting a bigger piece of wood into many smaller pieces, it is also called *fragmented incense* (瓣香/*ban-xiang*).

---

1. Incense fumes can drive away insects such as mosquitoes. People in India reportedly mixed oil with incense powder and applied it to their bodies so that insects would not bother them during long periods of sitting meditation.

Incense Vessel
(Incense Burner, Incense Thurible, Censer)

香 爐

Chn: *xiang-lu*

The incense vessel is used for holding incense that is burnt as an offering to Buddhist deities. Incense vessels can be made from different materials such as various types of metals or alloys, jade, porcelain, clay and stone. There exist various shapes and forms to the incense vessel but the most basic and commonly seen are those that are containers with a circular mouth. They may be flat-bottomed or be supported by three legs. Straight incense sticks are inserted vertically into ash or rice contained in the vessel. Another type is the lying incense vessel (臥香爐/*wo-xiang-lu*) which is oblong and round at both ends. It is also filled with ash and incense sticks are placed into the vessel in a lying horizontal position. This type of incense vessel also can have a lid with several openings through which the incense fumes can escape.

Another type is the hand-held incense holder (手爐/*shou-lu*) for use in special ceremonies (see *Hand-held Incense Holder*).

There are also incense vessels with special covers or lids that are used for burning wooden incense pieces. After pieces of incense wood are placed into the vessel along with incense powder that is then lit, the cover or lid is placed on top of the vessel and the incense smoke rises slowly through the many openings in the lid. The holes in the lid can be of various shapes and the lid may be mounted by an auspicious animal such as a lion or dragon. As clouds of gentle fragrance rise slowly through the lid and permeate the air, the environment becomes conducive to relaxation and contemplation and can induce feelings of sincere piety and devotion.

Lastly, there exist very large incense vessels that are found in front of temples in traditional monasteries. These huge incense vessels usually have a pagoda-like roof and are supported by three legs. Twin dragons may flank the sides of the huge incense vessel and auspicious symbols and writing may be a part of its design. These huge incense vessels are placed just outside the main temple hall and are called *treasure cauldrons* (寶鼎/*bao-ding*) in Chinese.

Oil Lamp

油 燈

Chn: *you-deng*

Skt: *dipa*

In Buddhism, lights (and therefore lamps) are used to symbolize the illumination of Wisdom that dispels ignorance. An oil-lamp is basically a bowl or some other vessel that is filled with oil and feeds one or several small burning flames. A circular float with a wick placed through its center is placed onto the surface of the oil. The top half-inch or so of the wick is left above the float exposed to air while the rest of the wick is inserted through the center of the float and submerged in the oil. The top of the wick burns as oil is absorbed upwards from the submerged part of the wick.

The oil-lamp can be of many forms. It can be very simple and basic like an ordinary glass bowl or it can be

something more artistic like a vessel designed like a lotus flower. In addition to being placed on tables in front of altars, oil-lamps can also be suspended from the ceiling in front of the shrine.

Similarly, lanterns, candles and other light producing objects are likewise used as symbols for the illumination of Wisdom in Buddhism. Many people nowadays place electric lamps and electric candles on altar tables for the same purpose.

Pagoda · Stupa

塔

Chn: *ta*
Jpn: *to*
Tib: *chorten*
Skt: *stupa*

The Chinese pagoda was originally based on the Indian stupa (舍利塔/*she-li-ta*), a reliquary used for storing the cremated remains and especially the sacred relics (舍利子/*she-li-zi*/*sharira*)[1] of the Buddha and other Buddhist monks. The stupa later also acquired additional forms of symbolism and became a sign of the Buddha's body (in Tibetan Buddhism, the Buddha's Mind) and

a representation of the Buddhist universe. Pilgrims and devotees usually walk around and circumambulate the stupa in a clockwise direction as a gesture of homage and also as an act of merit making.

As the prototype of the Indian stupa developed into the pagoda in China, its structure and design gradually changed and its form evolved into what is known today as the elegant architectural symbol popularly evocative of Far Eastern culture. The Chinese pagoda is characterized as being multi-storied, often eight-sided, with prominent exterior eaves at each level and a rising post at the very top.

A pagoda or stupa can be an actual tower or structure built on the grounds of a monastery or it can be a small scaled-down model that is placed on an altar or in a shrine as a religious symbol. While pagodas and  stupas, whether large or small, do not necessarily have to contain cremated remains or relics, some miniature stupas placed on altars and in shrines do hold sacred relics for veneration by devotees.

The pagoda as an iconographic attribute is seen in images of the Heavenly King Vaishravana[2] (see above) and is sometimes also seen in images of the Medicine Buddha.[3]

1. *Shariras*, or sacred relics, are jewel-like substances found in the cremated remains of those of high spiritual attainment (especially the Buddha). They can be of any color or shape, but they are often spherical and resemble pearls. These relics are said to be unbreakable, and stories abound of their ability to multiply themselves when venerated with sincerity and devotion. The existence of these relics, scientifically speaking, are an unexplained phenomenon, but are not uncommon throughout Buddhist circles.

   According to legend, 84,000 relics were found in the cremated remains of the Buddha after he passed into Parinirvana. These relics were subsequently enshrined in 84,000 stupas that were erected in his honor and spread across the land.

2. Vaishravana (多聞天王/*duo-wen-tian-wang*), Guardian of the North and one of the Four Heavenly Kings, is depicted as holding either a pagoda or a stupa in one of his hands.

3. In Chinese images of the Medicine Buddha Bhaisajyaguru (藥師佛/ *yao-shi-fo*), the pagoda sometimes rests on his two palms that are placed in his lap.

Prayer Cushion

蒲 團

Chn: *pu-tuan*

Prayer cushions provide a spot for people to kneel on and prostrate when praying or performing devotional

services and a place to sit when meditating. Prayer cushions can vary in size and shape. More older and traditional style prayer cushions are generally round in shape and filled with soft material inside.

Some of the more modern prayer cushions of today are generally square in shape and slightly angled on top

from front to back to facilitate a more comfortable postural alignment of a person's knees and back with his body when kneeling or prostrating.

In the temple hall during a ceremonial assembly, devotees will each take a spot before a cushion. Prayer cushions are usually arranged in two groups, one group to the left and one group to the right of the main altar. Traditionally, junior or female participants stood on the left, referred to as the *Western rank* (西單/*xi-dan*) while senior or male participants stood on the right, referred to as the *Eastern rank* (東單/*dong-dan*).

A much larger cushion, usually of a different color from the rest, often occupies the central position before the main altar. This center cushion is reserved for use by the abbot of the monastery and out of due respect, other monks or laypersons do not use this cushion.

Percussion Instruments Used for Chanting Accompaniment

Bell Bowl
Cymbals
Drum
Hand Chime
Hand-held Gong
Wooden Fish

Bell Bowl (Singing Bowl)

大 磬

Chn: *da-qing*

Jpn: *kinsu*

The bell-bowl is a musical implement made of bronze and shaped like a bowl. It is a major percussion instrument used in Chinese Buddhist chanting and is sounded throughout ceremonies to punctuate the reading

of religious texts. A short wooden rod is struck against the edge of the bell-bowl, creating a long resonating tone that floods the temple space with a field of acoustic energy. When heard, a settled and tranquil state of mind can be brought about.

There are various sizes to the bell-bowl that range from large to medium to small. The large bell-bowl is usually set on a stand near the main altar and is used when a large assembly of people chants in a large temple hall. Bell-bowls of a smaller size are generally used for chanting by smaller groups of people.

Cymbals

釕

Chn: *ke*

The cymbal is a musical instrument that is always played in conjunction with the hand-held gong (see *Hand-held Gong*) to accompany Chinese Buddhist chants and hymns. It is constructed of a round piece of copper or bronze alloy that has a central boss with a piece of cloth tied to the center hole to provide a grasp.

When the cymbals are played during a ceremony, each of the two pieces are held horizontally in each hand with the bottom piece facing up and the top piece facing down. Both pieces are stationed at the level of the solar plexus and are struck together maintaining its horizontal orientation.

Proper religious etiquette regarding the handling of ceremonial instruments, aimed at keeping dignity of manner during the performance of rituals, stipulates that the cymbals must be kept closed when they are not being played.

Drum

鼓

Chn: *gu*

The drum is struck in Buddhist temples to call people to the start of ceremonies and is also played in accompaniment to Buddhist chants and hymns.

There are various kinds of drums of different sizes. Sizes can range from very large drums that are placed atop special drum towers in traditional monasteries to small hand-held drums played by a monk when he chants in a group. More commonly seen in temple halls is the medium sized drum that is set on a stand paired with a small hanging bell that is played to accompany chanting during Buddhist ceremonies.

Hand Chime

引 磬

Chn: *yin-qing*

The hand chime is constructed of a small inverted bell attached to the top of a long handle. A long metallic needle of almost the same length, tied to the handle by a string, is used to strike the inverted bell to produce a high pitch ring.

This instrument is used to coordinate the vocal and physical actions of the assembly during Buddhist ceremonies. It is struck to keep rhythm during the chanting of certain passages of a religious text and also to signal when a transition is about to be made from one section of the text to the next. The chime is also used to let the assembly know when to bow and when to rise during the performance of prostrations.

In some cases, the use of the chime is also considered beneficial when used in chanting for those who are nearing death.[1]

1. In the Pure Land School, it is believed that those who are able to concentrate their thoughts single-mindedly on Amitabha Buddha at the time of death can achieve rebirth in his buddha-realm. Thus, it is customary practice for Chinese Buddhists to repeat the name of *Amitabha* at the bedside of someone who is dying. As an aid, the chime is sometimes employed in certain cases whilst chanting the sacred name. This is because when a person nears death, it is possible that he will see certain hallucinations and experience mental turbidity and confusion. The sound of the chime, clear and sonorous, can help him to remain clear-minded so that his thoughts can be focused wholly on Amitabha Buddha.

Hand-held Gong

鐺

Chn: *dang*

The hand-held gong is a musical instrument that is always played in conjunction with the cymbals (see *Cymbals*) to accompany Chinese Buddhist chants and hymns.

The hand-held gong is constructed of a bronze or copper alloy dish that is held within a circular metal frame by strings. These strings are attached from evenly spaced holes on the rim of the circular dish to the surrounding circular frame that is itself attached to a handle.

According to ceremonial etiquette, the hand-held gong is held in the left hand at face level and a miniature hammer held in the right hand is used to strike the gong.

Wooden Fish
(Wooden Block)

木魚

Chn: *mu-yu*

Jpn: *mokugyo*

The wooden fish is one of the most important tools used in Chinese Buddhist chanting. This instrument is made of wood and is round in shape. The exterior of the wooden fish is etched in design with features that resemble the eyes, scales, and tail of a fish representing ever-present awareness and diligence.[1]

The interior of the wooden fish is hollowed out so that when struck, it produces a dull wooden tone. A stick that has a small knob at one end is used to strike the wooden fish in a consistent rhythm

during scriptural recitation. The beat of the wooden fish poises the mind and establishes a tempo so that an assembly of people can chant in unison.

There are various sizes of the wooden fish that range from large to medium to miniature. The large wooden fish  is usually placed on a stand beside the main altar and is used when a large assembly of people chants in a large temple hall. A medium-size wooden fish is generally used for chanting by smaller groups and a miniature wooden fish is used as a hand-held instrument when it is inconvenient to use a stationary wooden fish (for example, when chanting while walking in procession).

---

1. Because fish do not have eyelids, their eyes always remain open, even when they sleep. Therefore, they symbolize to the Buddhist cultivator ever-present wakefulness and awareness. This state of constant mindfulness is an ideal sought after by Buddhist practitioners who strive to cultivate the mind. At all times, the cultivator must not let his guard down against allowing negative states of mind to arise.

Ceremonial & Ritual Objects

Cintamani Scepter
Fly Whisk
Hand-held Incense holder
Incense Tray
Incense-Flower Offering Dish
Mirror
Precept Ruler
Ritual Crown
Vajra Bell
Vajra Scepter

Cintamani Scepter (Jade Scepter)

如 意

Chn: *ru-yi*

Jpn: *nyo-i*

The cintamani-scepter is a ceremonial emblem of dignity and auspiciousness that is carried by Buddhist monks at important ceremonial events.

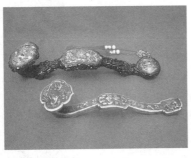

This ceremonial object is a finely carved piece of wood, jade, coral, or other precious or semi-precious substance. It is long and curved and is attached to a stylized headpiece. The center of the scepter sometimes contains a gem (or a replica of one) representing the cintamani.[1]

Based on various explanations that ascribe an origin to the cintamani-scepter, its design could have evolved from the form of an ancient scratching instrument, a certain type of short Chinese sword, a legendary fungus or plant that bestows longevity, or the tablets held by Chinese court officials when received in audience by the emperor.

---

1. In Buddhism, the *cintamani* (*chintamani*) (摩尼珠/ *mo-ni-zhu*) is the jewel that grants all wishes. According to legend, it finds its origin in the sea from the Dragon King. The cintamani is usually represented as a flaming pearl. It is eternally bright and radiant and thus is also a symbol of the Buddha and his Teachings.

Fly Whisk

拂　麈

Chn: *fu-chen*

Jpn: *hossu*

Skt: *chamara*

The fly-whisk is an honorific symbol of authority and dignity that is carried by a Buddhist monk presiding at important assemblies and ceremonial events.

The original usage of the fly-whisk was for scaring away insects and to clear away dust. Later, the religious symbolism of this object came to represent the sweeping away of impurities and defilements and the repelling of obstacles to the attainment of Enlightenment. Also, the fly-whisk can represent compassion and non-violence because by the action of swinging its whisks, tiny animals and insects are chased away and thereby protected from harm. The fly-whisk was also sometimes carried by Buddhist masters in Chan/Zen monasteries and therefore became an emblem of the *mind-to-mind transmission*[1] because it was passed down from the master to his Dharma heir.

The fly-whisk is constructed of animal hair, hemp, shredded fabric, or some other material that are bundled together and tied to a long thin handle.

The fly-whisk as an iconographic symbol can also be seen in Buddhist imagery and art. It is sometimes seen as an object carried by Bodhisattva Avalokiteshvara,[2] by attendants that stand next to a Buddhist deity,[3] and also by sages and other holy men (for example, the Buddha's disciple Ananda, shown at left).

1. The *mind-to-mind transmission* is the transmission of the realization of the Enlightened Mind, outside of words and scriptures, from the master to his disciple-successor. This has always been a hallmark of the Chan/Zen Buddhist lineage in ancient times (This does not mean, however, that Awakening can be *bestowed* by one person onto another. A cultivator necessarily must still personally work on introspection to achieve Awakening. The *transmission* mentioned here refers to the *sealing* or confirmation by the master of the disciple's true attainment of understanding).

2. In images of Bodhisattva Thousand-hands Avalokiteshvara/Guan-yin (千手觀音/*qian-shou-guan-yin*), the fly-whisk is carried in one of her many hands (see Plate 2).

3. See Plate 4 for a drawing of attendants that stand on both sides of a bodhisattva.

Hand-held Incense Holder

手 爐

Chn: *shou-lu*

The hand-held incense holder is a ritual implement used in special Buddhist ceremonies such as repentance rituals, ordination ceremonies, and other special rites such as *Inviting the Dharma Master*.[1]

The hand-held incense holder can be made of metal or wood. Its handle is generally curved and is attached to a headpiece that can have a special stylized design. An incense stick is inserted into the front headpiece and the implement is held with both hands with the headpiece in the front or it may also be held sideways with the headpiece on the left.

During a ceremony, the hand-held incense holder is held in front of the body when standing and at the level of the forehead when performing a half-bow or full prostration.

---

1. *Inviting the Dharma Master* (迎請法師/*yin-qing-fa-shi*) is a rite performed just before an important ceremony. Representatives from the assembly of participants in the event will ceremonially invite the officiating master(s) to the place of ritual.

Incense Tray

香 盤

Chn: *xiang-pan*

Jpn: *koban*

The incense tray is basically a rectangular tray with a piece of silk or satin cloth draped over its top and extended over the front. Buddhist symbols and other auspicious designs and writing are generally sewn onto the cloth. The incense tray serves to hold various implements for certain rituals and rites. These ritual items

can include an incense vessel, wooden incense pieces, offerings such as flowers, a small buddha or bodhisattva image, and other items.

The incense tray is commonly used in a ceremonial event where a group walks in procession. A tray bearer who stands in front carries the tray with both hands as he leads the group behind him.[1]

---

1. For example, during the *Three Steps One Prostration* (三步一拜/ *san-bu-yi-bai*) devotional rite, a tray bearer leading the pilgrimage group carries the incense tray as the group behind him continually prostrate to the ground for every three steps that are taken until a point of pilgrimage (usually a main shrine) is reached.

Incense-Flower Offering Dish

香 花 碟

Chn: *xiang-hua-die*

The incense-flower offering dish is a small round dish that is used for holding a symbolic offering of a flower and a piece of incense wood in certain Buddhist ceremonies.

Participants in the ceremony hold up the offering dish containing a flower and incense piece when the phrases of offering[1] are read aloud by the officiant monk or nun. The dish is typically held in the lotus finger mudra[2] using the left hand while the tips of the index and middle fingers of the right hand are held together and placed to the edge of the dish. Raised to the level of the forehead, the participant in the ceremony makes a mental contemplation of the offering.

1. For example, in the popular *Repentance of Great Compassion Ceremony* (大悲懺法會/*da-bei-chan-fa-hui*), the offering dish is held up as the phrases of offering are read aloud: *All in this assembly, each one kneeling, holding incense and flower in adornment, give offering in accord with the Dharma; May this fragrant flower cloud fully pervade the realms of the ten directions. May all buddha-lands one by one be adorned with boundless fragrance. May the Bodhisattva Path be fulfilled and the buddha-fragrance be achieved.*
(是諸眾等，各各胡跪，嚴持香花，如法供養：
願此香花雲，遍滿十方界，一一諸佛土，
無量香莊嚴，具足菩薩道，成就如來香 。)

2. The lotus finger mudra (蓮花指/*lian-hua-zhi*) is formed by extending the thumb, index and small fingers of the hand upwards while keeping the middle and ring fingers in a tightly closed position. In Buddhism, mudras are ritualistic hand gestures that encode special meanings.

Mirror

鏡

Chn: *jing*

Jpn: *kagami*

Skt: *adarsha*

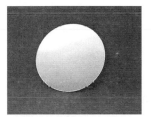

The mirror is a symbol of the clear and luminous nature of the Buddha's Enlightened Mind. It is round, and therefore perfect, and it reflects everything around it while it itself remains unstained and unaffected, just like the nature of the Enlightened Mind which spontaneously reflects and perceives all phenomena.

The mirror is a ritual object used during *opening light* (開光/*kai-guang*) ceremonies where monks hold up a round

mirror to ceremonially "open" or "bring to life" a new Buddha statue for worship. The round mirror can also be found situated behind the heads of buddha and bodhisattva statues where they symbolize the Mind of Enlightenment or the divine halo. Amongst the many sacred objects held by the Bodhisattva Thousand-hands Avalokiteshvara/Guan-yin, the *precious mirror* (寶鏡/*bao-jing*) is also one of them.

The mirror has always been a favorite symbol of the mind's true nature (which is none other than Enlightenment itself). In the story of the contest between Shen-xiu/Shen-hsiu (神秀) and Hui-neng (惠能), they both showed their understanding of Chan/Zen[1] to the Fifth Patriarch by each writing a stanza.

Shen-xiu wrote: *The body is like a bodhi tree, the mind a mirror bright. Carefully we wipe it constantly, so that no dust can alight.*[2]

Hui-neng saw Shen-xiu's stanza. He then wrote: *In essence there is no bodhi tree, nor a stand of a mirror bright. Since in essence all is void, where can the dust alight?*[3] Hui-neng won the seal as the Sixth Patriarch of Chan Buddhism in China.

---

1. Chan/Zen is direct awakening to the mind's true enlightened nature. Lu K'uan Yu defines Chan/Zen in its more narrower meaning as the *name of mind* in his *Ch'an and Zen Teaching* series.

2. The English version of the stanza here is a slight revision based on the one in *The Sutra of Hui Neng: Sutra Spoken by the 6th Patriarch on the High Seat of The Treasure of the Law* published by Hong Kong Buddhist Book Distributor Press, p.15.

3. Ibid., p.18.

Precept Ruler

戒 尺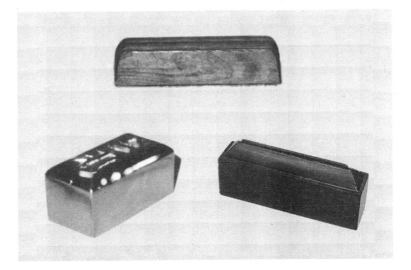

Chn: *jie-chi*

The precept ruler is essentially a single or double block of rectangular wood. Traditionally for the double block precept ruler, a horizontal grasp was attached to the top piece so that it can be lifted and struck against the lower piece to produce a loud clapping sound. During certain ceremonial events, the precept ruler is used by a monk to signal that he is about to speak or read aloud certain parts of a text.

Nowadays, the precept ruler may only be a single block of wood or metal. This simplified precept ruler is slapped against a table for the same purpose and effect.

The use of the precept ruler is often seen in precept transmission ceremonies[1] or when a monk reads religious text during a ritual or as part of giving formal Buddhist teachings.

---

1. During a ceremony for precept transmission, the precept ruler is sounded for each precept that is read aloud by the precept transmission master to the postulants. Precept transmissions are given to those who choose to receive and uphold various rules and observances. He or she may be taking precepts to live a more disciplined life as a lay Buddhist or to become an ordained monastic. Buddhist precepts include the Five Precepts (五戒/*wu-jie*) for laypeople, the Ten Precepts (十戒/*shi-jie*) for novice monks and nuns, the Two Hundred Fifty Precepts for fully ordained monks (比丘二百五十戒/*bi-qiu-er-bai-wu-shi-jie*), and the Five Hundred Precepts for fully ordained nuns (比丘尼五百戒/ *bi-qiu-ni-wu-bai-jie*).

Ritual Crown
(Vairochana Hat)

毗 盧 帽

Chn: *pi-lu-mao*

The ritual crown is a ceremonial hat often worn by monks when performing rites involving the esoteric use of mantras and visualizations. The monk who wears the crown assumes the role of the *Vajra-master* (金剛上師/*jin-gang-shang-shi*) and must be skilled in esoteric ceremony such as deliverance rituals (超度/*chao-du*) for the dead or the more grand-scale *Release of the Burning Mouths* (放燄口/*fang-yan-kou*). These ceremonies involve spiritually transforming (and multiplying) food offerings into nectar (甘露/*gan-lu*/*amrta*) or into a form edible for departed spirits (e.g., in deliverance ceremonies)[1] or for *hungry ghosts* (e.g., in the burning mouths ceremony).[2]

The crown has five pentagonal-shaped pieces that are situated on the rim of the crown and each of the five pieces contains an image of one of the *Five Dhyani*

Buddhas[3] (one of which is Buddha Vairochana, the central figure of the five buddhas, thus giving the name *Vairochana Hat* in Chinese). A vertical top-piece rises from the center of the crown and two long pendants hang down from both sides of the hat.

---

1. Departed spirits are those that have died and are in the *bardo* (中陰/*zhong-yin*), the state in-between death and the next rebirth, lasting a maximum period of forty-nine days. Such spirits are mental-bodies that feed on smell and the essence of food.

2. In the Buddhist teachings, there are six realms in the cycle of transmigration. They are 1) gods or heavenly beings (天人/ *tian-ren/deva*), 2) fighting demigods or demons (阿修羅/ *a-xiu-luo/ashura*), 3) humans (人/*ren*), 4) animals (畜生/ *chu-sheng*), 5) hungry ghosts (餓鬼/ *e-gui/preta*), and 6) hell-beings (地獄/*di-yu*).
   Hungry ghosts are spiritual entities that suffer constantly from hunger and thirst, unable to eat or drink because they have needle-size throats and any food that they attempt to take turns into fire or molten iron. Rebirth into this woeful state is a result of having too much greed. The *Release of the Burning Mouths* ceremony, popular especially during the seventh Chinese lunar month, is performed to temporarily relieve these unfortunate beings of their suffering and misery.

3. The *Five Dhyani Buddhas* (五方佛/*wu-fang-fo*) are:

Akshobhya Buddha (阿閦埤佛/*a-chu-pi-fo*) of the East. His corresponding wisdom is *Adarshana-jnana* (大元鏡智/*da-yuan-jing-zhi*), the great mirror wisdom of reflection.

Ratnasambhava Buddha (寶生佛/bao-sheng-fo) of the South. His corresponding wisdom is *Samata-jnana* (平等性智/*ping-deng-xing-zhi*), the wisdom of universality and impartiality.

Amitabha Buddha (阿彌陀佛/*a-mi-tuo-fo*) of the West. His corresponding wisdom is *Pratyavekshana-jnana* (妙觀察智/*miao-guan-cha-zhi*), the wisdom of profound insight and observation.

Amoghasiddhi Buddha (不空成就佛/*bu-kong-cheng-jiu-fo*) of the North. His corresponding wisdom is *Krtyanusthana-jnana* (成所作智/*cheng-suo-zuo-zhi*), the wisdom of perfection for the welfare of self and others.

Vairochana Buddha (毗盧遮那佛/*pi-lu-zhe-na-fo*) of the Center. His corresponding wisdom is *Dharmadhatu-prakrti-jnana* (法界體性智/*fa-jie-ti-xing-zhi*), the wisdom of the embodied nature of the *Dharmadhatu*.

Vajra[1] Bell (Diamond Bell, Hand Bell)
金 剛 鈴

Chn: *jin-gang-ling*

Jpn: *kongo-rei*

Tib: *drilbu*

Skt: *ghanta*

The vajra-bell and the vajra-scepter (see next entry), commonly referred to as the *bell and vajra*, are principal ritual instruments of Esoteric Buddhism.[2] Although these two objects are employed mainly in Tibetan Buddhism, they are not entirely unknown in Chinese Buddhism because they are also used in certain Chinese Buddhist ceremonies that are esoteric in nature.[3] The vajra-bell and the vajra-scepter are traditionally always to be used together. The vajra-bell and scepter can be made of various metals or alloys. During esoteric Buddhist rituals, the Buddhist master wields these instruments in his hands as he recites liturgical chants and performs hand movements endowed with mystical meaning.

The vajra-bell and scepter, when paired together, represent the union of the feminine and masculine principles, the Purpose and Method, Transcendental Wisdom and Compassion.

The vajra-bell, as an individual symbol, can stand for the Buddhist doctrine of impermanence and transience.[4] The vajra-bell originated in India as it was already a symbol used by Vedic divinities in pre-Buddhist times.

The handle of the bell is surmounted by half of a vajra-scepter. The design of the bell's vajra handle (i.e., the number of prongs and its style) matches the vajra-scepter that it is used with. So for example, the commonly seen 5-prong handle vajra-bell matches the 5-prong vajra-scepter that it is paired with.

The vajra-bell is also often seen in Buddhist imagery and art. For example, Bodhisattva Thousand-hands Avalokiteshvara/Guan-yin carries the vajra-bell in some of her representations.[5]

1. *Vajra* is an Indian Sanskrit word meaning *adamantine*. It denotes something that is indestructible, impenetrable and indivisible. It is perfect and immaculate and cannot be blemished nor destroyed in any way but has the power to cut through anything. The concept of the *Vajra* is used to describe the Buddhist Doctrine because it is also perfect, indestructible, and has the power to cut through all obstacles. This word is sometimes translated as *diamond* by Western authors.

2. Esoteric (or Tantric) Buddhism commonly refers to Vajrayana Buddhism (金剛乘/*jin-gang-sheng*/Adamantine or Diamond Vehicle) which is popularly known as the form of Buddhism practiced in Tibet. Other esoteric Buddhist schools or ones that incorporate esoterism in their practice are Japanese *Shingon* Buddhism (眞言宗/*zhen-yan-zong*/True Word School), and Chinese *Tian-tai* and its Japanese counterpart, *Tendai* Buddhism (天台宗/*tian-tai-zong*/Celestial Platform School).

3. Historically, Chinese Buddhism included ten different schools, one of which was the *Chen-yen/Zhen-yan* (True Word; i.e. *mantras* or *dharanis*) esoteric school. Although considered no longer extant, this school is the forerunner of *Shingon* Buddhism, an esoteric school practiced widely today in Japan. Esoteric elements that exist today in Chinese Buddhist ritual are remnants of this ancient esoteric school.

4. Worldly phenomena is just like the sound of the bell because the bell's sound is heard but gradually fades away. So it is the same with all conditioned phenomena-they are impermanent, empty and ultimately lack substantial reality.

5. See Plate 2 for example.

Vajra Scepter
(Diamond Scepter, Thunderbolt Scepter)

金 剛 杵

Chn: *jin-gang-chu*
Jpn: *kongo-sho*
Tib: *dorje*
Skt: *vajra*

The vajra-scepter is a symbol of the transcendental power of the Buddha's Law[1] (see also the previous entry on *Vajra Bell* for a general introduction and on the specific meaning of the vajra-scepter when paired together with the vajra-bell). Some sources attribute the origin and evolution of the vajra-scepter to the ancient Indian symbol of the thunderbolt or lightning-strike, a weapon of the Vedic god Indra.[2]

The vajra-scepter is a double-ended instrument with both ends that are structurally alike. The two ends of the vajra-scepter, being identical, symbolize the unified duality of the transcendental and phenomenal worlds, the Buddha-realm and the realm of sentient beings.

On most commonly seen vajra-scepters, the stylized prongs at both ends of the vajra-scepter curve and meet a straight central prong. On these scepters, the straight central prong is surrounded by the other exterior inward-curving prongs whose tips are fused with the central prong. In some other varieties, the surrounding exterior prongs are not fused at the tips but are left splayed. Some scepters may even lack the central prong and only have the outer exterior prongs. There exist many different scepters of varying styles and each type possesses different attributes and symbolisms. The overall design of the scepter and the number of prongs it can have all depends on its style and purpose.

The number of prongs on the ends of the vajra-scepter stand for certain attributes and ideas in the Mahayana Buddhist teachings. For example, the one prong of the single-prong scepter represents the *Dharmadhatu*.[3] The three prongs of the 3-prong scepter represent the *Three Mysteries*.[4] The five prongs of the commonly seen 5-prong scepter represent the *Five Dhyani Buddhas* and their corresponding wisdom energies.[5]

 The vajra-scepter is also present in Buddhist imagery and art. The scepter is sometimes carried by the Bodhisattva Avalokiteshvara/Guan-yin[6] and also by many other Buddhist deities.

---

1. The Buddha's Law (*Buddhadharma*) is like the *Vajra*. It is perfect, indestructible, and cuts through all obstacles on the path to Enlightenment.

2. Indra (因陀羅/*yin-tuo-luo*) is the Hindu god of the natural elements. He was later adopted into Buddhism as a Dharma-protecting deity (i.e., guardian deities that defend the Buddhist Law).

3. The *Dharmadhatu* (眞法界/*zhen-fa-jie*) is the *unifying underlying spiritual reality, regarded as the ground or cause of all things, the absolute from which all proceeds* (Soothill, William E. *A Dictionary of Chinese Buddhist Terms*).

4. The *Three Mysteries* (三密/*san-mi*) refer to body (身/*shen*), mouth (口/*kou*), and mind (意/*yi*). In esoteric Buddhist practice, *mudras* (mystical hand gestures) correspond to body (physical actions), *mantras* or *dharanis* (vocal multi-syllabic formulas or incantations) correspond to mouth (speech), and meditation and visualization correspond to mind.

5. The *Five Dhyani Buddhas* (五方佛/*wu-fang-fo*) and their corresponding wisdoms are:

Akshobhya Buddha (阿閦埤佛/*a-chu-pi-fo*) of the East.
His corresponding wisdom is *Adarshana-jnana* (大圓鏡智/*da-yuan-jing-zhi*), the great mirror wisdom of reflection.

Ratnasambhava Buddha (寶生佛/*bao-sheng-fo*) of the South.
His corresponding wisdom is *Samata-jnana* (平等性智/*ping-deng-xing-zhi*), the wisdom of universality and impartiality.

Amitabha Buddha (阿彌陀佛/*a-mi-tuo-fo*) of the West.
His corresponding wisdom is *Pratyavekshana-jnana* (妙觀察智/*miao-guan-cha-zhi*), the wisdom of profound insight and observation.

Amoghasiddhi Buddha (不空成就佛/*bu-kong-cheng-jiu-fo*) of the North.
His corresponding wisdom is *Krtyanusthana-jnana* (成所作智/*cheng-suo-zuo-zhi*), the wisdom of perfection for the welfare of self and others.

Vairochana Buddha (毗盧遮那佛/*pi-lu-zhe-na-fo*) of the Center.
His corresponding wisdom is *Dharmadhatu-prakrti-jnana* (法界體性智/*fa-jie-ti-xing-zhi*), the wisdom of the embodied nature of the *Dharmadhatu*.

6. See Plates 2 and 3 for example.

Objects & Tools Used in the Monastery

Convocating Board
Giant Bell
Giant Drum
Meditation Stick

Convocating Board

板

Chn: *ban*

The convocating board is a wooden board or metal plate that is struck with a stick or hammer in a rhythmic manner for sounding an auditory signal to assemble people in Buddhist monasteries. The convocating board can be made of bronze, iron, or wood.

There are many different shapes to the convocating board that vary according to style and purpose. For example, the board that calls people to meals (齋板 /zhai-ban) is generally shaped like a fish. The wake-up board (起板 /qi-ban) sounded in the morning, often seen today, is generally shaped like a rectangle with the two top corners missing[1] (not shown here). Other varieties also exist depending on the tradition and purpose of use.

1. This shape follows the traditions of the *Lin-ji/Lin-chi* (臨濟) and *Cao-dong/Tsao-tung* (曹洞) sects of the Chan school.

Giant Bell

大 鐘

Chn: *da-zhong*

The giant temple bell is traditionally a very important tool in Buddhist monasteries. In many of the larger monasteries, it is hung in a bell tower and a long piece of wood that is suspended horizontally next to the bell is used to strike it. Giant bells are usually cast with designs consisting of auspicious symbols, religious text, or other writing.

In the monastery, the bell master, a monk or nun responsible for sounding the giant bell, will toll it at certain times of the day. Generally, the giant bell is always sounded in the morning before devotional services and in the evening after devotional services. Verses that accompany the tolling of the bell are recited as the bell is struck. Different schools of Buddhism may sound the bell in different ways but it is generally struck a total of 108 times-one toll for each of the 108 vexations of Man.[1]

The full deep resonance of the giant bell, when heard, can settle and clear the mind, induce feelings of reverence and devotion, and call attention to mindfulness. In accordance with Buddhist codes of conduct, one must not lie down when the bell is sounded but should instead remain upright and have the mind brought to focused attention.

It is said: *When the bell is sounded in Buddhist temples, evil demons will tremble with fear and the sinners in hell are relieved temporarily of their suffering.*

---

1. It is said that Man has 108 vexations (煩惱/*fan-nao*/*klesha*) which are the mental passions, defilements and afflictions that bind them to samsara. The number 108 is symbolic because this number has a magico-mystical significance in Far-Eastern traditions.

Giant Drum

大 鼓

Chn: *da-gu*

See entry under *Drum*.

Meditation Stick
(Chan-board, Wake-up Stick)

禪 板

Chn: *chan-ban*

Jpn: *kyosaku · shippei*

The meditation stick, named *chan¹-board* in Chinese, is a flat wooden board carried by the meditation teacher or proctor in a meditation hall to help sitting meditators keep proper physical posture and to wake those that are falling asleep. The meditation stick in Chinese Buddhism is generally shaped like a sword with a wide blade whose tip does not, however, terminate in a point but is flat.

During formal meditation sessions, a monk walks quietly around the meditation room with the meditation stick in hand and observes each meditator. If he finds anyone dozing off or using incorrect body posture, a nudge or strike with the meditation stick, often to the shoulders, is used to help correct the condition. Also, an unenlightened student can be brought to spiritual awakening if he is struck at just the right moment with the meditation stick when used by a skillful Buddhist master. The meditation stick also figures as an emblem of discipline and authority in Chinese Buddhist monasteries.

It is said: *When struck by the meditation stick, negative karma is reduced, wisdom is gained and realization will be achieved.*

---

1. The term *Chan* is the Chinese transliteration of the Indian Sanskrit *Dhyana* which means *concentration* or *meditation*. It is better known in the West by its Japanese name *Zen*.

Ceremonial Attire & Other Objects

Almsbowl

Hai-qing Robe

Kasaya Robe

Man-yi Robe

Mendicant's Staff

Patch Mat

Rosary

Almsbowl (Begging Bowl)

鉢

Chn: *bo*

Jpn: *hachi*

Skt: *patra*

The almsbowl was originally one of the Eighteen necessary items of the traveling Buddhist monk[1] and is  carried to collect food and other offerings given by lay-devotees. The almsbowl is made of metal or  earthenware and its color is traditionally a dark shade like black, gray, or crimson. The size of the almsbowl is suppose to conform to restrictions of maximum and minimum volume and the mouth of the almsbowl is generally smaller than the widest part of its body so that food is better contained and spillage prevented.

A legend that describes the origin of the use of the almsbowl by Buddhist monks runs as follows: Trapusa and Bhalika, two merchants traveling with a caravan, spotted the Buddha along the way and so halted their journey.

They presented food to the Buddha as an offering but the Buddha, wanting to set an example for his order of monks, said that he could not accept the food because he did not have an almsbowl. Immediately, the Four Guardian Kings of the four cardinal directions[2] each made a gift of an almsbowl made of a precious material to the Buddha. The Buddha, however, refused the gift because the bowls were made of precious substances. The Four Guardian Kings then each presented the Buddha again with four different bowls, this time made of ordinary stone. The Buddha then accepted and taking the four bowls, magically consolidated them into a single almsbowl and received the food offered by the two merchants.

The almsbowl is often seen in Buddhist imagery and its iconographic significance came to be a symbol of monasticism, renunciation and even the Buddha's Law. The almsbowl is prevalent in images of the historical Buddha Shakyamuni[3] and can also be seen in images of Amitabha[4] and Avalokiteshvara.[5]

1. See Appendix for a list of the 18 required items that had to be carried by a traveling Buddhist monk of the Chinese Mahayana tradition in ancient times.

2. The Four Guardian Kings (四大天王/*si-da-tian-wang*/*chatus-lokapala*) are: 1) Dhritarashtra of the East (東方持國天王/*dong-fang-si-guo-tian-wang*), 2) Virudhaka of the South (南方增長天王/*nan-fang-seng-chang-tian-wang*), 3) Virupaksha of the West (西方廣目天王/*xi-fang-guang-mu-tian-wang*), 4) Vaishravana (or Dhanada) of the North (北方多聞天王/*bei-fang-duo-wen-tian-wang*).

3. See Plate 1 for example.

4. In sitting images of Buddha Amitabha (阿彌陀佛/*a-mi-tuo-fo*/Buddha of Infinite Light), the almsbowl is held in both hands that are placed in the lap.

5. In images of Bodhisattva Thousand-hands Avalokiteshvara/Guan-yin (千手觀音/*qian-shou-guan-yin*), the almsbowl is carried in one of her many hands (see Plate 2).

Hai-qing Robe

海 青

Chn: *hai-qing*

The hai-qing (pronounced "hye-ching") robe is the basic ceremonial robe of Chinese Buddhism. Ordained monks and nuns wear the hai-qing robe beneath the kasaya robe (see *Kasaya Robe*) while laypersons that have formally taken religious precepts[1] wear it beneath the man-yi robe (see *Man-yi Robe*). Buddhist laypersons that have not formally taken any religious precepts wear the hai-qing robe by itself without any outer robe.

The hai-qing robe is probably evolved from the Chinese dress style of the Han[2] and Tang[3] dynasties. The hai-qing robe worn by monks and nuns can be black, yellow or ochre in color. When worn by a lay-Buddhist, it is generally black in color.

The robe's collar is made of three unequal lengths of cloth that are sewn and layered on top of one another. These three layers of cloth represent in Buddhism the *Three Treasures*.[4] The collar encircles the back of the neck and goes down the front of the chest. As part of its

design, there is also a rectangular area on the collar near the front of the chest that has many visible lines of thread. One explanation for this design is that it stands for the story of the Buddhist pilgrim *Sudhana*.[5] Another explanation is that when one commits a transgression of the precepts, one is expected to remove one of the threads from the collar to confess one's mistake.

The very wide sleeves of the hai-qing robe are also very unique in that the actual opening at the ends of the sleeves are only approximately one-fourth of the sleeves' actual breadth. The origin for this unique design of the sleeves comes from the story of monk *Bao-zhi*.[6]

According to Buddhist normative etiquette, the hai-qing robe is always handled with care and respect because it is a sanctified robe used solely in Buddhist rituals. According to Buddhist protocol, appropriate physical deportment and proper ways of donning, taking off, and folding up of the robe are always to be observed.[7]

1. A layperson that holds religious precepts is somebody that has taken the Three Refuges *and* also at least the Five Precepts.

2. Han Dynasty (漢朝) 206 BCE to 220 CE.

3. Tang Dynasty (唐朝) 618 to 907 CE.

4. The *Three Treasures*, also called the *Triple Jewel* or *Triple Gem* (三寶/*san-bao/triratna*), are 1. the Buddha, 2. the Dharma (teachings of the Buddha), and 3. the Sangha (the ordained Buddhist Order).

5. The youth *Sudhana* (善財童子/*shan-cai-tong-zi*) is the pilgrim who traveled to seek out 53 teachers in his quest for Enlightenment. It is said that the collar of the hai-qing robe has 53 lines of thread (in theory at least) in tribute to this story. The story of Sudhana is told in the chapter of the Avatamsaka Sutra entitled *Entering the Dharma Realm* (大方廣佛華嚴經入法界品/*da-fang-guang-fo-hua-yan-jing-ru-fa-jie-pin*)

6. During the reign of Emperor Liang Wudi (梁武帝), there was a monk known as *Chan Master Bao-zhi* (寶誌禪師). The emperor's wife, Xi-shi (希氏), heard of the master's extraordinary reputation and wanted to put him to the test to see if he possessed the spiritual power of foreknowledge. She schemed to invite the master to a meal but would secretly serve him meat-filled buns. Knowing that Chinese monks were bound by the strict observance of vegetarianism, she smiled at the fact that the master also could not refuse an offering made to him by the royal household. When Master Bao-zhi received the invitation, he already knew of her plan through his spiritual powers so he devised a way to solve the impending problem. He had the ends of his sleeves closed up leaving an opening only large enough for his hands to fit through. The rest of the empty space in his wide sleeves would afford him a place to hide vegearian buns that he would bring along with him. The master went to meet Xi-shi on the appointed day and as the meat-filled buns were served to him, he dropped them into his one empty sleeve and took out his own buns from the other sleeve to eat. From that day on, Xi-shi held the master in great esteem.

7. Ceremonial etiquette is aimed at ensuring that all manner of conduct and physical movement involved in the performance of a ritual are dignified and solemn. Also, the ways regarding the proper manner of handling the robe are attempts to foster the development of awareness and mindfulness which are qualities that all Buddhist practitioners strive to cultivate.

Kasaya Robe (Patch Robe, Monastic Toga)

袈裟

Chn: *jia-sha*
Jpn: *kesa*
Tib: *namjar*
Skt: *kasaya (kashaya)*

The kasaya robe is the ceremonial outer robe of the Chinese Buddhist monastic. This is not to be confused with a monk's ordinary everyday robe. The kasaya robe, together with the hai-qing robe (see *Hai-qing Robe*), make up the formal ceremonial attire of Chinese monks and nuns. The kasaya robe is also called the *patch robe* because it is made by sewing together several, individual pieces or patches of cloth.[1] This robe is also known as a *Field of Blessings Garment* (福田衣/*fu-tian-yi*) in Chinese because its patchwork design is likened to the neat, rectangular image of rice paddy fields and indicative of the idea that the monastic sangha[2] is the supreme source of planting the seeds of blessings.

The kasaya robe in China is classified into 3 types: the *wu-yi* (五衣/vestment of five pieces), *qi-yi* (七衣/vestment of seven pieces), and *da-yi* (大衣/great vestment of many pieces). This categorization is based on the total number of patches of cloth that the robe is comprised of.[3] These three categories of kasaya robes are also called the *Three Garments* (or *Three Robes*) and were originally one of the Eighteen necessary items that had to be kept by a traveling Buddhist monk.[4]

Depending on the nature of the function or event that a monk attends, he appropriately wears one of the three different types of kasaya robes for ceremonial attire. The *wu-yi* was originally worn in ancient times when performing general or ordinary tasks in the monastery (today however, the *wu-yi* is hardly ever worn for this purpose anymore). The *qi-yi* is worn when attending official functions like receiving Buddhist teachings or chanting during ceremonies. The *da-yi*, which itself can be divided into 9 different grades, is reserved for when a monk publicly lectured on scriptures, expounded Buddhist teachings, or when officiating at ceremonies. Generally, only ranking monks and nuns in the monastery wore the *da-yi* because it was only they who gave teachings and officiated at ceremonies. The color of the kasaya robe also depends on its classification and grade. Generally, in China, the *wu-yi* and *qi-yi* are brown or yellow while the *da-yi* is yellow or red. The appropriate robe is always worn concordant with the nature of the religious event and is also generally indicative of the monk's hierarchical rank in the monastery or Buddhist order.

The proper way of wearing the Chinese kasaya robe is on top of the basic hai-qing robe. In the traditional manner that Indian Buddhist monks wore their robes, the Chinese kasaya robe is draped across the body over the left shoulder and under the right arm, leaving the right shoulder exposed. The kasaya robe is secured by a hook and ring located near the front of the left shoulder. According to ceremonial protocol, the monk always follows a particular procedure in flawless fashion when putting on and taking off his kasaya robe facing away from any Buddhist images nearby.

Also of interest is that aside from the traditional types of kasaya robes mentioned above, there have also been special *da-yi* robes like the purple kasaya robe and the gold-embroidered kasaya robe worn by eminent monks in the past.[5] These special robes, however, are rarely seen in modern times.

---

1. The robes originally worn by Indian monks in the Buddha's time were made by sewing together old pieces of discarded cloth. Later, monastic robes were no longer required to be made from discarded cloth but they still had to be sewn together from separate patches of cloth. Similarly, the Chinese kasaya robe is also made from separate, although not necessarily different, patches of cloth. The reasoning behind this is that monks are not suppose to wear garments that were valuable. A piece of cloth that was cut into several smaller pieces and then sewn back together again was deemed to be degraded in worth and thus to be more in accord with the ideal of renouncing the world and its luxuries.

2. The *sangha*, defined specifically, is the monastic Buddhist order of ordained monks and nuns. This is different from its more broader meaning which refers to the community of general Buddhist practitioners.

3.

Type of Kasaya Robe	Lengths of Cloth Sewn Together	No. of Patches Each Length is Consisted of	Total No. of Patches
Wu-yi	5	2 (1 long, 1 short)	10
Qi-yi	7	3 (2 long, 1 short)	21
Da-yi	9	3 (2 long, 1 short)	27
	11	3 (2 long, 1 short)	33
	13	3 (2 long, 1 short)	39
	15	4 (3 long, 1 short)	60
	17	4 (3 long, 1 short)	68
	19	4 (3 long, 1 short)	76
	21	5 (4 long, 1 short)	105
	23	5 (4 long, 1 short)	115
	25	5 (4 long, 1 short)	125

4. See Appendix for a list of the 18 required items that had to be carried by a traveling Buddhist monk of the Chinese Mahayana tradition in ancient times.

5. Even though Buddhism originally placed strict emphasis on simplicity in regards to monastic attire, valuable robes such as the purple kasaya robe and the gold-embroidered kasaya robe were presented as gifts to eminent monks by patrons of the imperial household as gestures of reverence.

Man-yi Robe

縵 衣

Chn: *man-yi*

The brown color man-yi (pronounced "mon-yee") robe is the Buddhist layperson's ceremonial outer robe that looks very similar to the kasaya robe worn by Chinese monks. The man-yi robe is worn in the same manner as the monastic kasaya robe (see *Kasaya Robe*) on top of the basic hai-qing robe (see *Hai-qing Robe*).

Laypersons who have officially taken the *Three Refuges*[1] and the *Five Precepts*[2] are qualified to wear the man-yi robe in addition to the basic hai-qing robe.[3] The man-yi robe, unlike the monastic kasaya robe, does not follow the patchwork design (i.e., neat rectangular patches of cloth that are sewn together to form one larger piece of cloth, symbolic of renunciation and monasticism) because lay-Buddhists are not considered full religious renunciates. Therefore, the layperson's man-yi robe is made from a single, uncut whole piece of cloth. But aside from this distinction, it is similar in almost every other way to the monastic kasaya robe worn by monks and nuns.

1. The *Three Refuges* (三皈依/*san-gui-yi*/*trisarana*) are: 1) taking refuge in the Buddha, 2) taking refuge in the Dharma (Buddhist Teachings), and 3) taking refuge in the Sangha (order of ordained monks and nuns).

2. The *Five Precepts* (五戒/*wu-jie*/*pancha-veramani*), strictly speaking, should be observed by every Buddhist. They are: 1) not to take life, 2) not to steal, 3) not to engage in sexual misconduct, 4) not to commit negative speech (i.e., lying, harsh language, speaking ill of others, idle gossip), and 5) not to take intoxicants.

3. The hai-qing robe can be worn by anyone who has taken the *Three Refuges*.

Mendicant's Staff (Pilgrim's Staff)

錫 杖

Chn: *xi-zhang*

Jpn: *shakujo*

Skt: *khakkara*

The mendicant's staff was originally one of the Eighteen necessary items of the traveling Buddhist monk.[1] The staff is made of lightweight metal or wood and is topped by a stylized finial made of metal from which metallic rings hang.

When begging for alms in front of a house or requesting admission to a monastery for lodging in

ancient times, the monk would announce his presence by shaking his staff. The rings on the staff would strike against one another and produce a metallic rattling noise. The staff also functioned as a walking stick and the monk shook the staff to ward off animals that may pose a threat to him when he traveled and to scare away small animals and insects that might be in his path so that he would not accidentally trample on them. In some schools of Esoteric Buddhism, the mendicant's staff is also seen as a tool of magical agency where it is used as an instrument in exorcisms of demons and spirits.

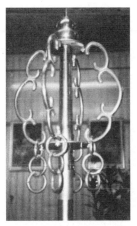

In China, the commonly seen design of the metal finial on the head of the staff has a miniature knob at the very peak in the form of a three-level pagoda that represents the *Threefold Learning*.[2] Below the knob is a set of either two or four stylized arches that are attached to the staff like handles. A set of two arches stands for the *Two Forms of Truth*[3] and a set of four arches stands for the *Four Noble Truths*.[4] A series of three interlinking metallic rings hang from each arch. Six rings (three rings that hang from each of two arches) stand for the *Six Paramitas*[5] and twelve rings (three rings that hang from each of four arches) stand for the *Twelve Nidanas*.[6]

Today, the mendicant's staff is used more as a ceremonial symbol than as a practical tool. Buddhist monks carry the staff at important ceremonial events as a sign of monasticism and spiritual authority.

The mendicant's staff can also be seen in Buddhist imagery and art. For example, a figure well known as a bearer of the mendicant's staff is Bodhisattva Kshitigarbha[7] (see left). The staff can also be seen in certain representations of Bodhisattva Avalokiteshvara[8] and it is even carried by certain attendants[9] that stand next to a buddha or bodhisattva.

---

1. See Appendix for a list of the 18 required items that had to be carried by a traveling Buddhist monk of the Chinese Mahayana tradition in ancient times.

2. The *Threefold Learning* (三學/*san-xue*) are 1. Discipline (戒/*jie/shila*), 2. Concentration (定/*ding/dhyana*), and 3. Wisdom (慧/*hui/prajna*).

3. The *Two Forms of Truth* (二諦/*er-di*) are Conventional/Relative Truth (俗諦/*su-di/samvrti-satya*) and Ultimate/Absolute Truth (眞諦/*zhen-di/paramartha-satya*).

4. The *Four Noble Truths* (四聖諦/*si-sheng-di/chatus-arya-satya*) are 1. the Truth that life is suffering (苦/*ku*), 2. the Truth that the accumulation of desire is the cause of suffering (集/*ji*), 3. the Truth that the ending of suffering is possible (滅/*mie*), and 4. the Truth that the way leading to the ending of suffering is the Eightfold Path (道/*dao*).

5. The *Six Paramitas* (六波羅蜜/*liu-bo-luo-mi*) are 1) Charity (布施/*bu-si*/*dana*), 2) Discipline (持戒/*chi-jie*/*shila*), 3) Patience (忍辱/*ren-ru*/*kshanti*), 4) Diligence (精進/*jing-jin*/*virya*), 5) Concentration (禪定/*chan-ding*/*dhyana*), and 6) Wisdom (智慧/*zhi-hui*/*prajna*).

6. The *Twelve Nidanas* (十二因緣/*shi-er-yin-yuan*/Twelve Links of Causation) are 1) Ignorance (無明/*wu-ming*/*avidya*), 2) Action (行/*xing*/*samskara*), 3) Consciousness (識/*shi*/*vijnana*), 4) Name & Form (名色/*ming-se*/*nama-rupa*), 5) Six sense organs (六入/*liu-ru*/*sadayatana*), 6) Contact (觸/*chu*/*sparsha*), 7) Sensation (受/*shou*/*vedana*), 8) Desire (愛/*ai*/*trshna*), 9) Grasping (取/*qu*/*upadana*), 10) Existence (有/*you*/*bhava*), 11) Birth (生/*sheng*/*jati*), and 12) Aging & Death (老死/*lao-si*/*jara-marana*).

7. Kshitigarbha (地藏/*di zang*/Earth Store) is the bodhisattva who vowed never to enter Final Enlightenment until all sentient beings in hell are delivered. In images of Kshitigarbha, the mendicant's staff is seen in his right hand while his left hand holds the cintamani pearl. It is said that in his mission to save those who have been reborn in hell, he uses his staff to break open the gates of the underworld.

8. In images of Bodhisattva Thousand-hands Avalokiteshvara/Guan-yin (千手觀音/*qian-shou-guan-yin*), the mendicant's staff is carried in one of her many hands (see Plate 2).

9. See Plate 4 for a drawing of attendants that stand on both sides of a bodhisattva.

Patch Mat (Monastic Mat)

具・尼師壇

Chn: *ju · ni-shi-tan*

Skt: *nisidana/nishidana*

The patch mat was originally one of the Eighteen necessary items to be carried by a traveling monk.[1] Buddhist monks originally used the patch mat as a floor covering when sitting or lying on the ground. In Chinese Buddhism, the mat is also used for performing prostrations during devotions and ceremonies. Today, the patch mat is more symbolic than practical in usage because the mat serves as a ceremonial emblem of Buddhist monasticism. In special Chinese Buddhist ceremonies, the monk unfolds his mat and places it on his prayer cushion before performing prostrations on it.

The patch mat, like the kasaya robe (see *Kasaya Robe*), follows the patchwork design of being made from several smaller and separate pieces of cloth.[2] In the Chinese Buddhist tradition, the patch mat looks like a large piece of cloth that is segmented into several geometric parts of different colored areas.

1. See Appendix for a list of the 18 required items that had to be carried by a traveling Buddhist monk of the Chinese Mahayana tradition in ancient times.

2. A piece of cloth that is sewn back together from several smaller patches of cloth is considered to be devalued in worth as compared to a single whole piece of cloth. Thus, the patchwork design represents renunciation of and detachment from worldly luxury and mundanity, an attitude that all Buddhist monks keep.

Rosary
念 珠

Chn: *nian-zhu*[1]

Jpn: *nenju*

Skt: *mala*

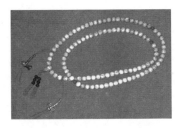

The rosary is an important implement used by Buddhist practitioners.[2] The rosary is used to facilitate in counting when a person recites the name of a buddha, bodhisattva, or a mantra.[3] The practitioner either silently recites with the mind or vocally recites with the mouth while the hand fingers the rosary beads to keep track of the number of repetitions. Rosaries usually have a head bead that is slightly larger in size than the rest of the other beads. This head bead is used as a starting point and benchmark for counting a full rotation of the entire rosary. Some larger rosaries (like the 108-bead

rosary) also possess three *spacing* or *demarcation beads* (界珠/*jie-zhu*) that may be slightly smaller and different in color from the rest of the beads. These demarcation beads, together with the starting head bead, divide the rosary into four equal segments.

Some rosaries also have two short strings of tinier beads that branch off the main rosary to serve as counter-beads. When one full circle of the rosary has

been reached in recitation, a counter-bead is moved up the string to mark a full cycle.

Many Buddhist practitioners keep a rosary readily in-hand as a reminder to be constantly mindful of the Buddha, to always uphold a pure and spiritual mind-set and to always maintain assiduousness in recitation practice.

Rosary beads can be made from a number of different materials including various kinds of wood (e.g., sandalwood), seed (e.g., bodhi, lotus, rudraksha), semi-precious and precious material (e.g., coral, agate, lapiz lazuli, crystal), and even bone.

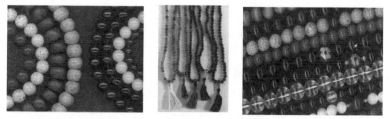

The number of beads that traditionally can be found on a rosary number 108, 54, 42, 27, 21, or 18 beads. These numbers stand for various concepts in the teachings of Mahayana Buddhism and are outlined here as follows:

No. of Beads	Significance
108	108 Vexations of Man[4]
	108 Deities of the Vajradhatu[5]
54	10 Faiths[6]
	10 Abodes[7]
	10 Practices[8]
	10 Transferences of Merit[9]
	10 Grounds[10]
	4 Virtuous Roots[11]
	54 (In Total)
42	10 Abodes
	10 Practices
	10 Transferences of Merit
	10 Grounds
	2 Supreme Forms of Buddha-Enlightenment[12]
	42 (In Total)
27	18 Stages of Learning[13]
	9 Grades of Non-Learning[14]
	27 (In Total)
21	10 Grounds
	10 Paramitas[15]
	1 (the 21st stage of Buddha-attainment)[16]
	21 (In Total)
18	18 Realms[17]
	18 Arhats[18]

The rosary is also commonly seen in Buddhist imagery and art. For instance, we can see in certain images of Bodhisattva Avalokiteshvara/Guan-yin that she holds in her hands a string of rosary beads.[19]

---

1. Literally *remembrance beads* in Chinese.

2. The rosary is accorded greater importance in Northern Buddhism (i.e., Mahayana and Vajrayana) than in Southern Buddhism (i.e., Theravada) due to the difference in emphasis of practice between the two schools.

3. Constant practice in recitation purifies negative karma and clears away karmic obstacles such as illness and calamities. More importantly though, diligent practice can open up the mind to wisdom and develop advanced stages of concentration.

4. It is said that Man has 108 vexations (煩惱/*fan-nao*/*klesha*) which are the mental passions, defilements and afflictions that bind them to samsara. The number 108 is symbolic because this number has a magico-mystical significance in Far-Eastern traditions.

5. The *vajradhatu* (金剛界/adamantine or diamond realm) represents the realm of active Enlightenment.

6. The *Ten Faiths* (十信/*dasha-shraddha*) are the 1st through 10th in the 52 stages of the development of a bodhisattva into a buddha (according to the Tian-tai and Hua-yan schools). They are: 1) Mind of faith (信心), 2) Mind of remembrance (念心), 3) Mind of diligence (精進心), 4) Mind of wisdom (慧心), 5) Mind of concentration (定心), 6) Mind of non-retrogression (不退心), 7) Mind of protection of the Dharma (護法心), 8) Mind of the transference of merit (迴向心), 9) Mind of discipline (戒心), and 10) Mind of resolution (願心).

7. The *Ten Abodes* (十住/*dasha-sthiti*) are the 11th through 20th in the 52 stages of the development of a bodhisattva into a buddha. They are: 1) Abode of spiritual resolve (發心住), 2) Abode of mental control (治地住), 3) Abode of cultivation (精進住), 4) Abode of noble birth (生貴住), 5) Abode of perfect means (方便具足住), 6) Abode of the correct mind (正心住), 7) Abode of non-retrogression (不退住), 8) Abode of immortal youth (童眞住), 9) Abode of the Dharma prince (法王子住), and 10) Abode of investiture/annointment (灌頂住).

8. The *Ten Practices* (十行) are the 21st through 30th in the 52 stages of the development of a bodhisattva into a buddha. They are: 1) Practice of joyful service (歡喜行), 2) Practice of beneficial service (饒益行), 3) Practice of non-resentment (無瞋恨行), 4) Practice of boundless service (無盡行), 5) Practice of perseverant service (離痴亂行), 6) Practice of limitless manifestations (善現行), 7) Practice of unimpeded activity (無著行), 8) Practice of exaltation of the paramitas among sentient beings (尊重行), 9) Practice of perfection of the Dharma by complete virtue (善法行), and 10) Practice of manifestation of True Reality in all phenomena (眞實行).

9. The *Ten Transferences of Merit* (十迴向/*dasha-parinamana*) are the 31st through 40th in the 52 stages of the development of a bodhisattva into a buddha. They are: 1) Transference of delivering sentient beings and parting with their characteristics (救護一切衆生離衆生相迴向), 2) Transference of indestructibility (不壞迴向), 3) Transference of equalization to all buddhas (等一切佛迴向), 4) Transference of omnipresence (至一切處迴向), 5) Transference of the store of infinite merit (無盡功德藏迴向), 6) Transference of compliance with the equality of virtuous roots (隨順平等善根迴向), 7) Transference of compliance with non-discriminatory observation of all sentient beings (隨順等觀一切衆生迴向), 8) Transference of the mark of True Reality (眞如相迴向), 9) Transference of unrestricted liberation (無縛無著解脫迴向), and 10) Transference of the boundlessness of the ten dharma realms (等法界無量迴向).

10. The *Ten Grounds* (十地/*dasha-bhumi*) are the 41st through 50th in the 52 stages of the development of a bodhisattva into a buddha. They are: 1) Ground of joyfulness (歡喜地/*pramudita-bhumi*), 2) Ground of purity (離垢地/*vimala-bhumi*), 3) Ground of illumination (發光地/*prabhakari-bhumi*), 4) Ground of radiant wisdom (焰慧地/*archismati-bhumi*), 5) Ground of overcoming difficulties (極難勝地/*sudurjaya-bhumi*), 6) Ground of direct presence (現前地/*abhimukhi-bhumi*), 7) Ground of proceeding afar (遠行地/*durangama-bhumi*), 8) Ground of immovability (不動地/*achala-bhumi*), 9) Ground of virtuous wisdom (善慧地/*sadhumati-bhumi*), and 10) Ground of assembling the Dharma clouds (法雲地/*Dharmamegha-bhumi*).

11. The *4 Virtuous Roots* (四善根/*chatus-kushala-mula*) are: 1) Warming (暖): Like a burning fire, one identifies one's mind with that of Buddha-Enlightenment. 2) Summit (頂): Relying on self-mind to win Enlightenment, one progresses to the summit like climbing a mountain. The body enters the Void and leaves behind only minor traces of obstruction. 3) Endurance (忍): One maintains the sphere of non-grasping while also enduring with detachment to the non-grasping mind. 4) World-Victorious dharma (世第一法): One does not abide in delusion nor Awakening nor anywhere in between. One has not yet attained to the beginning stages of the transcendental/supramundane realm but has reached the ending stages of the worldly/mundane realm. Even though outflows of vexations still exist, one has achieved *Worldly Victory*.

12. The Two Supreme Forms of Buddha-Enlightenment are *Universal Enlightenment* (等覺) and *Wonderful Enlightenment* (妙覺). They are respectively the 51st and 52nd stages in the final development of a bodhisattva into a buddha.

13. The *Eighteen Stages of Learning* (十八學/*astadasha-saiksa*) refer to the stages where one has not yet reached to the level of an arhat and thus still requires study and instruction.

14. The *Nine Grades of Non-Learning* (九無學/*navan-asaiksa*) refer to the nine grades of arhats who have completed their course of learning and are no longer subjected to delusion. Thus, they no longer require ordinary learning and are beyond the need for ordinary study.

15. The *Ten Paramitas* (十波羅蜜/*dasha-paramita*) are made up of the regular six paramitas plus four additional ones. They are: 1) Charity (布施/*dana*), 2) Discipline (持戒/*shila*), 3) Patience (忍辱/*kshanti*), 4) Diligence (精進/*virya*), 5) Concentration (禪定/*dhyana*), 6) Wisdom (智慧/*prajna*), 7) Expediency (方便/*upaya*), 8) Vows (願/*pranidhana*), 9) Strength in resolution (力/*bala*), and 10) Knowledge (智/*jnana*).

16. One of the stages of Buddha-attainment or reward as contrasted with the causation stage.

17. The *Eighteen Realms* or *Elements of Perception* (十八界/*astadasha-dhatu*) are the six senses (六根界/*sad-indriya*), their six sense-objects (六塵界/*sad-guna*), and their six sense-perceptions (六識界/*sad-vijnana*). They are: 1) eye (眼/*chaksur-indriya*), 2) ear (耳/*shrotra-indriya*), 3) nose (鼻/*ghrana-indriya*), 4) tongue (舌/*jihva-indriya*), 5) body (身/*kaya-indriya*), 6) mind (意/*mano-indriya*), 7) form (色/*rupa*), 8) sound (聲/*shabda*), 9) smell (香/*ghanda*), 10) taste (味/*rasha*), 11) touch (觸/*sprastavga*), 12) thought (法/*dharma*), 13) eye consciousness (眼識/*chaksur-vijnana*), 14) ear consciousness (耳識/*shrota-vijnana*), 15) nose consciousness (鼻識/*ghrana-vijnana*), 16) tongue consciousness (舌識/*jihva-vijnana*), 17) body consciousness (身識/*kaya-vijnana*), and 18) mind consciousness (意識/*mano-vijnana*).

18. According to Buddhist legend, there were 16 (and then later 18) legendary arhats. They are:

1. Pindolabharadvaja (賓度羅跋囉惰闍尊者/賓頭盧頗羅墮誓尊者)
2. Kanakavatsha (迦諾迦伐磋尊者)
3. Kanakabharadvaja (迦諾迦跋釐惰闍尊者)
4. Suvinda (蘇頻陀尊者)
5. Nakula (諾距羅尊者)
6. Bhadrapada (跋陀羅尊者)
7. Karika (迦理迦尊者)
8. Vajraputra (伐闍羅弗多羅尊者)
9. Supaka/Svaka (戍博迦尊者)
10. Pandaka (半托迦尊者)
11. Rahula (囉怙羅尊者)
12. Nagashena (那伽犀那尊者)
13. Ingata (因揭陀尊者)
14. Vanavashin (伐那婆斯尊者)
15. Ajita (阿氏多尊者)
16. Cudapandaka/Suddhipandaka (注茶半托迦尊者)
17. Nandimitra (慶友尊者); Dharmatrata in Tibetan Buddhism (達摩多羅・西藏所傳)
18. Mahakashyapa (摩訶迦葉尊者); Monk Mahayana in Tibetan Buddhism (大乘和尚・西藏所傳)

19. In images of the Bodhisattva Thousand-hands Avalokiteshvara/ Guan-yin, Four-arms Guan-yin, and Chundi Guan-yin, the rosary is present in one of her many hands (see Plates 2 and 3 for example).

Appendix

The 18 necessary items that had to be carried by a traveling Buddhist monk of the Chinese Mahayana tradition in ancient times were:

1. Buddha image
2. Bodhisattva image
3. Sutra text (Buddhist scripture)
4. Vinaya text (Code of discipline for monastics)
5. The Three Robes (Skt: *kasaya/kashaya*)
6. Mendicant's staff (Skt: *khakkara*)
7. Almsbowl
8. Incense vessel
9. Hammock
10. Patch mat (Skt: *nisidana/nishidana*)
11. Pincer (grasping device)
12. Fire producer
13. Dagger
14. Cloth/towel
15. Water strainer
16. Water bottle
17. Poplar brush (toothbrush)
18. Soda ash (soap)

Selected Bibliography

Chen yi xiao ju shi bian. Fo xue chang jian ci hui. Da sheng jing she yin jing hui yin xing.
陳義孝居士編／佛學常見詞彙／大乘精舍印經會印行

Lu, K'uan Yu. *Ch'an and Zen Teaching.* Maine: Samuel Weiser, Inc., 1993.

Soothill, William Edward. *A Dictionary of Chinese Buddhist Terms.* Great Britain: Curzon Press, 1995.

The Sutra of Hui Neng: Sutra Spoken by the 6th Patriarch on the High Seat of The Treasure of the Law. Hong Kong: Hong Kong Buddhist Book Distributor Press.

Xiang yun fa shi zhu. Fo jiao chang yong bai qi qi wu fu zhuang jian shu. Ci xin fo jing liu tong chu yin xing.
祥雲法師著／佛教常用唄器、器物、服裝簡述／
慈心佛經流通處印行

Dedication of Merit

May any merit resulting from this work be wholly dedicated to all sentient beings. May each and every one of them be always separated from suffering and sorrow and the causes of suffering and sorrow. May they all enter upon the path of self-cultivation and eventually achieve liberation.